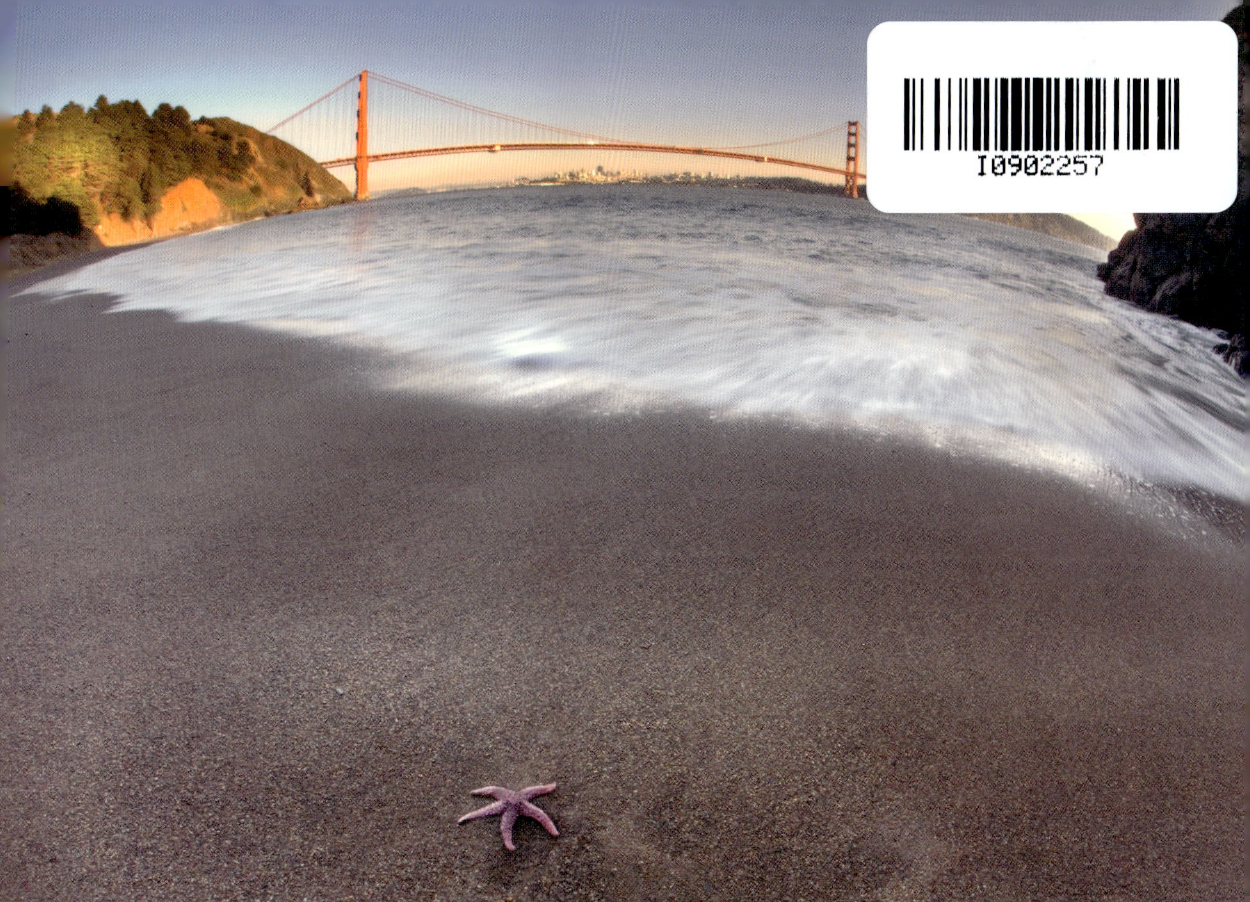

Point Reyes and the Marin Headlands

Starfish and Bridge—Kirby Cove, Golden Gate National Recreation Area, CA

CAMERON + COMPANY PETALUMA CA 94952 WWW.CAMERONBOOKS.COM

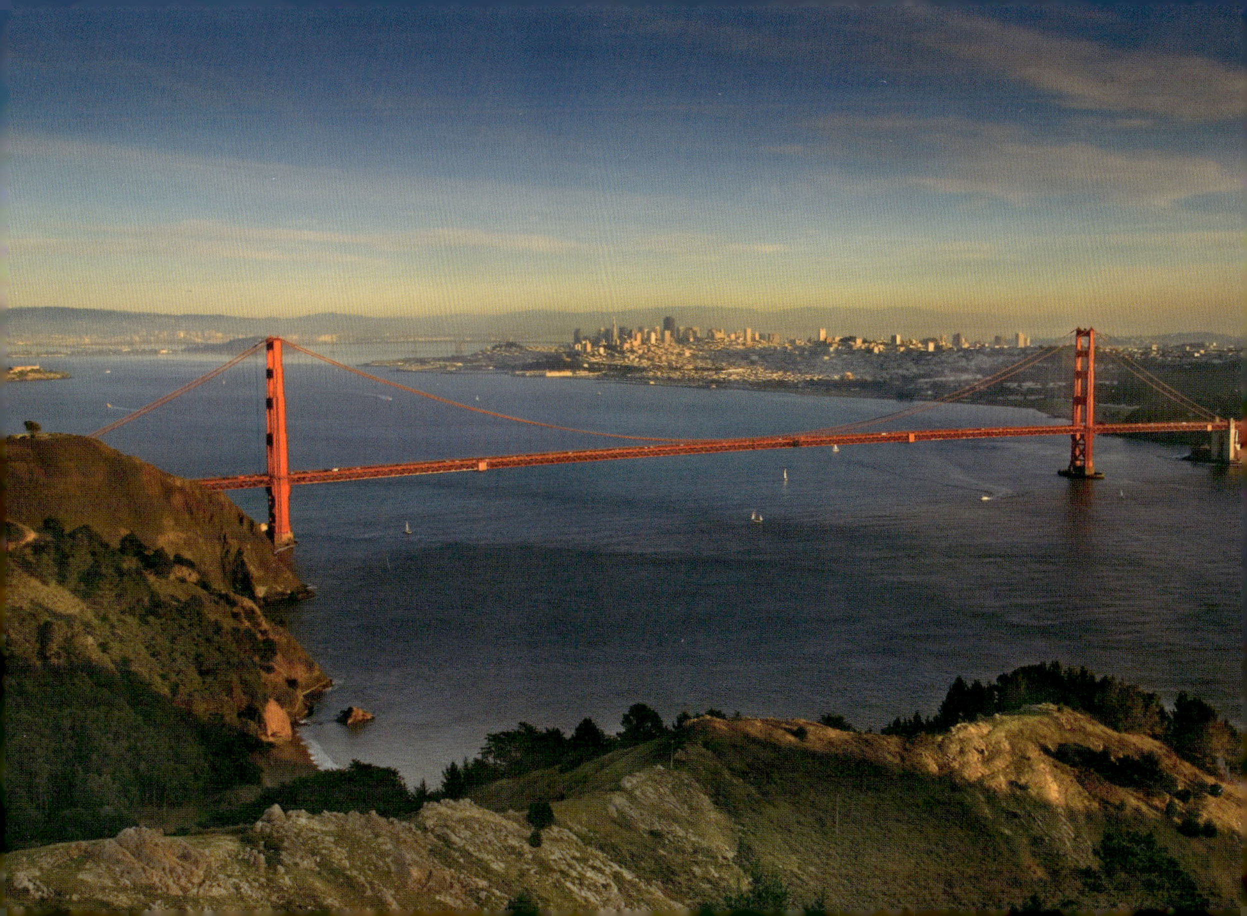

Point Reyes and the Marin Headlands

City by the Bay—San Francisco and the Golden Gate Bridge from the Marin Headlands, Golden Gate National Recreation Area, CA

CAMERON + COMPANY PETALUMA CA 94952 WWW.CAMERONBOOKS.COM

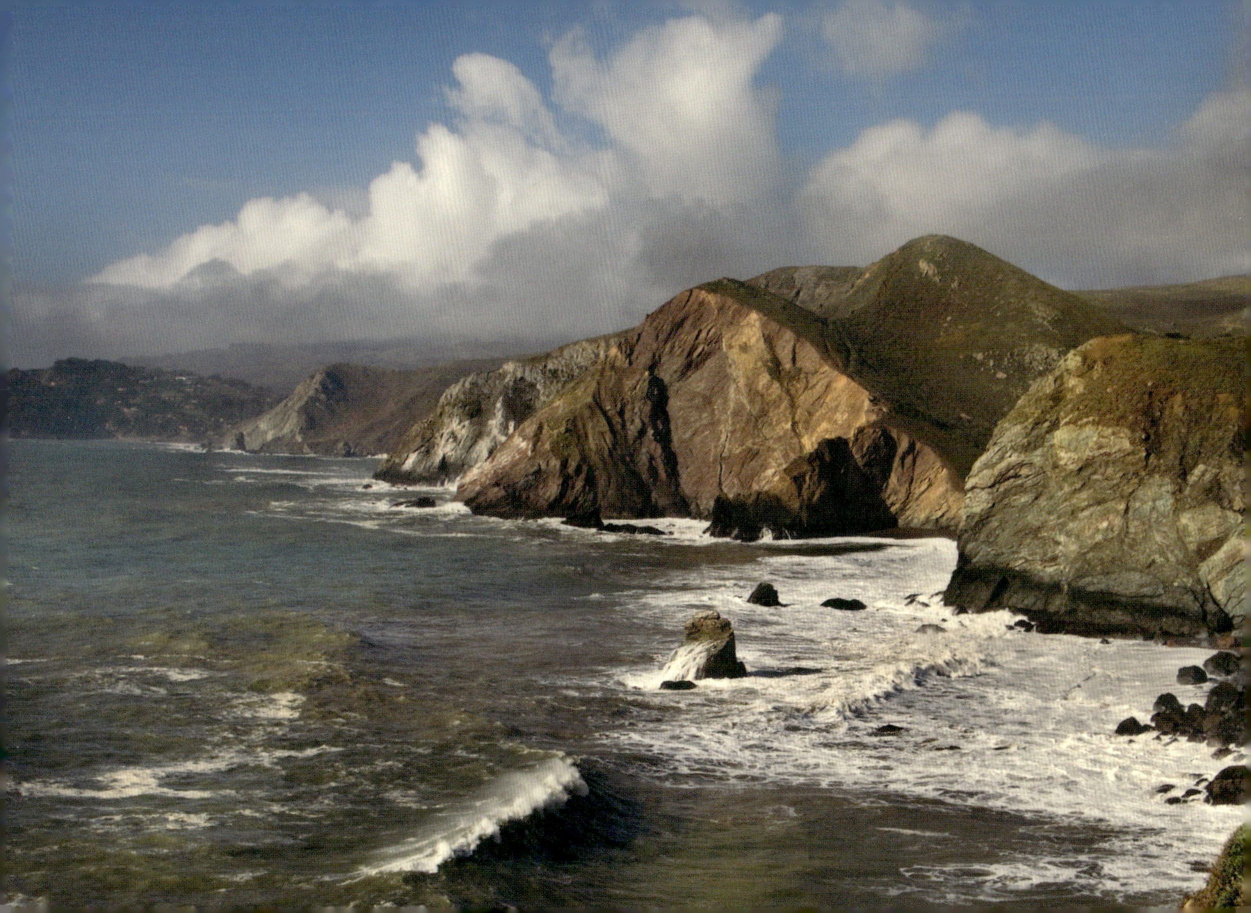

Point Reyes and the Marin Headlands

Marin Headlands—Tennessee Beach and the rugged Marin coastline, Golden Gate National Recreation Area, CA

CAMERON + COMPANY PETALUMA CA 94952 WWW.CAMERONBOOKS.COM

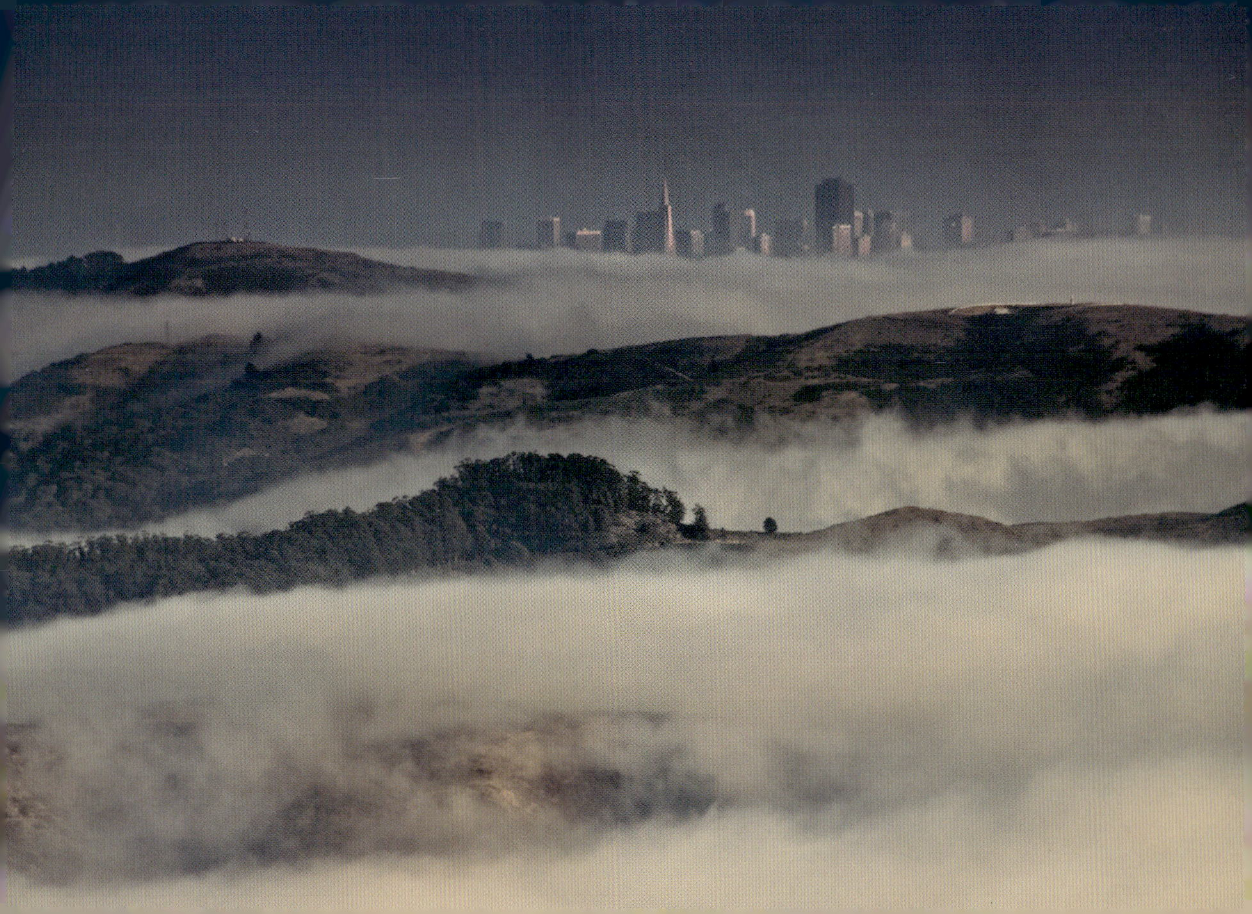

Point Reyes and the Marin Headlands

Marin Headlands and San Francisco from Mount Tamalpais,
Tamalpais State Park, CA

CAMERON + COMPANY PETALUMA CA 94952 WWW.CAMERONBOOKS.COM

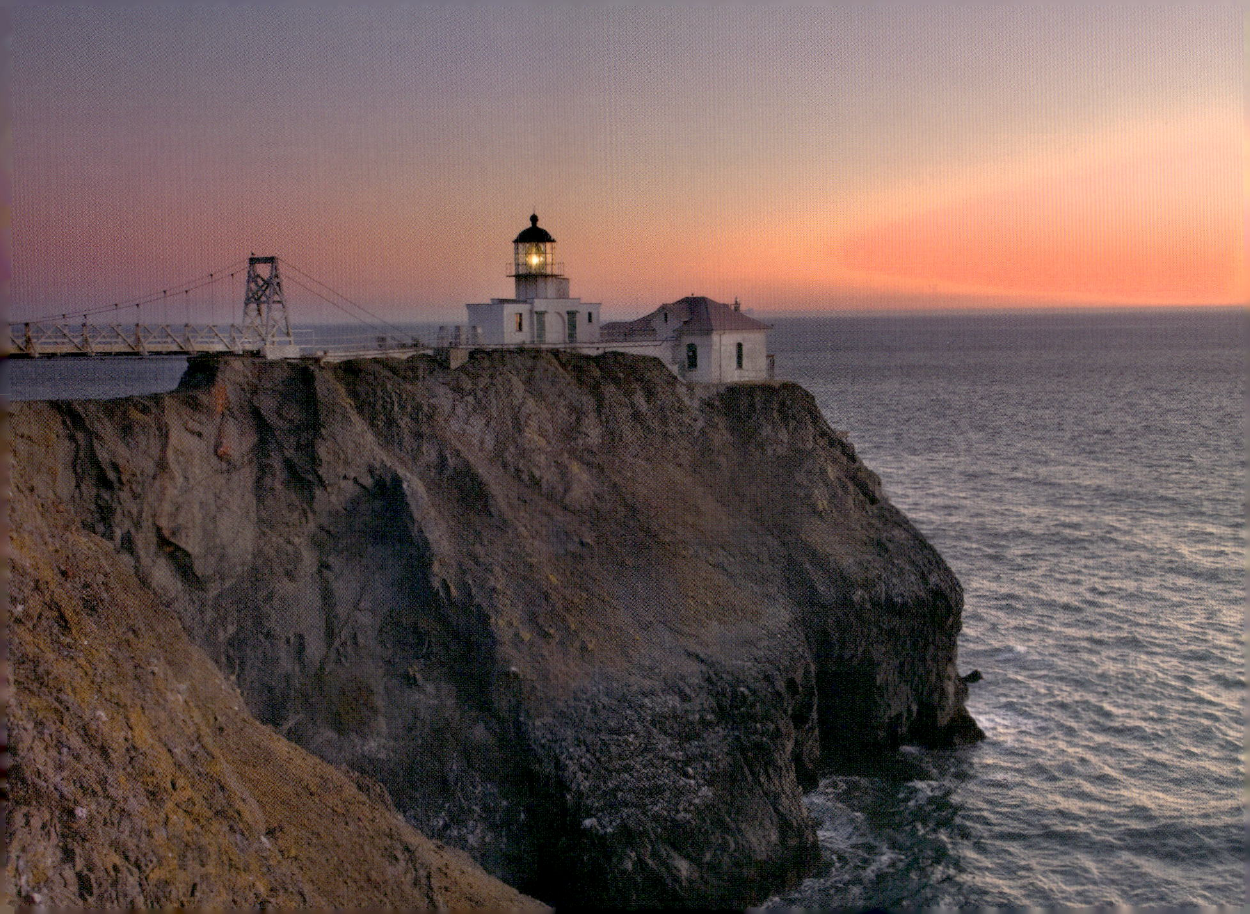

Point Reyes and the Marin Headlands

Point Bonita Lighthouse, Golden Gate National Recreation Area, CA

CAMERON + COMPANY PETALUMA CA 94952 WWW.CAMERONBOOKS.COM

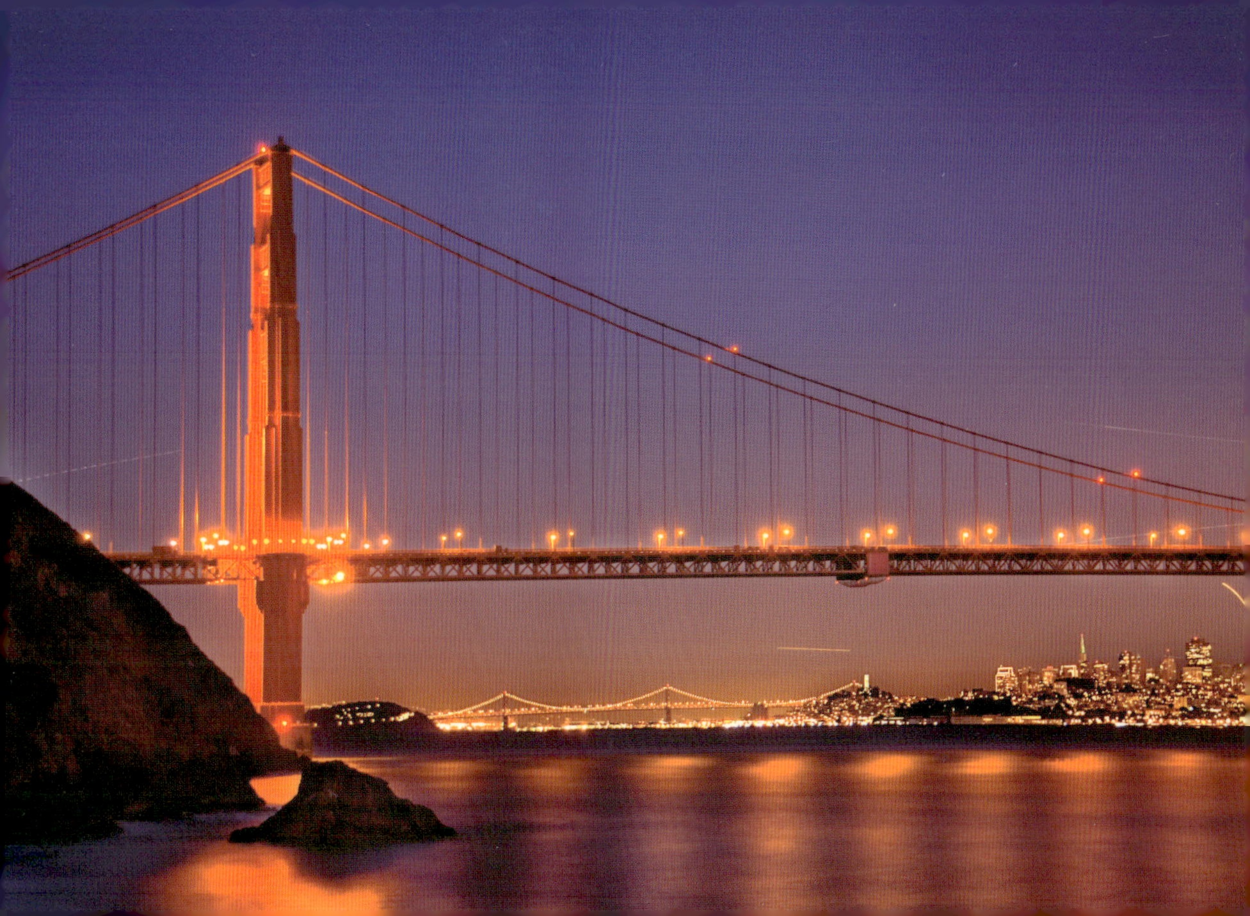

Point Reyes and the Marin Headlands

Two Bridge View—The Bay Bridge and Golden Gate Bridge from Kirby Cove in the Marin Headlands, Golden Gate National Recreation Area, CA

CAMERON + COMPANY PETALUMA CA 94952 WWW.CAMERONBOOKS.COM

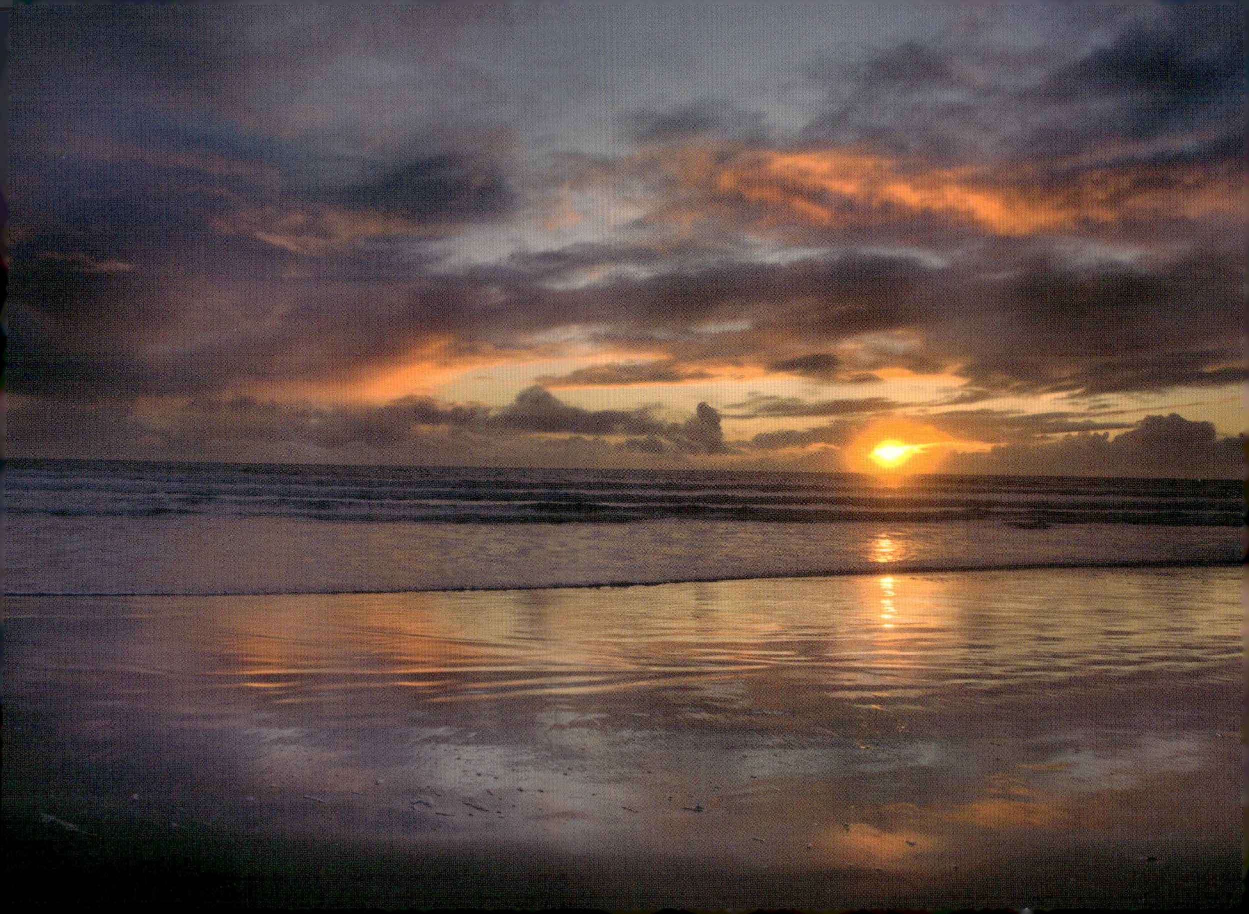

Point Reyes and the Marin Headlands

Stinson Beach Sunset, Golden Gate National Recreation Area, CA

CAMERON + COMPANY PETALUMA CA 94952 WWW.CAMERONBOOKS.COM

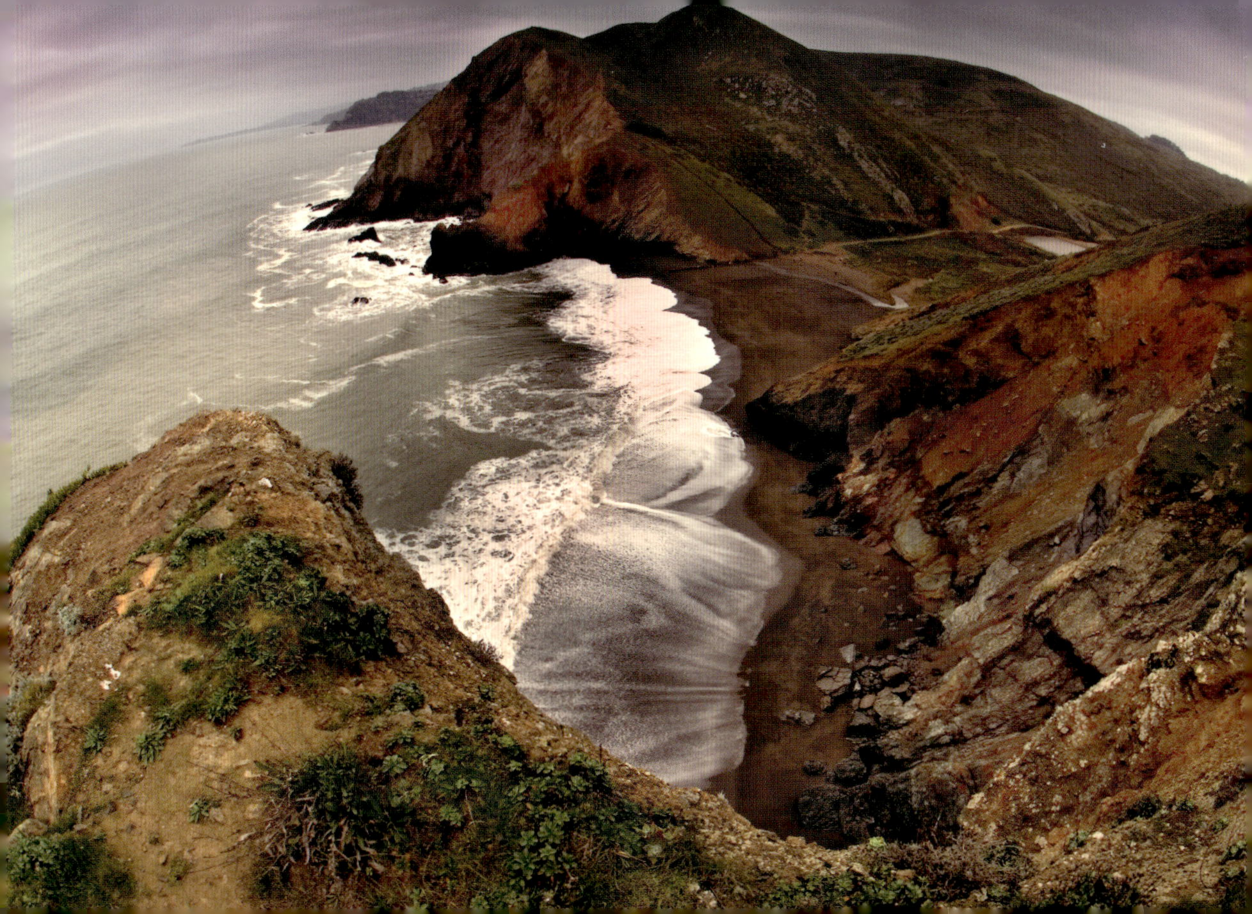

Point Reyes and the Marin Headlands

Tennessee Cove, Golden Gate National Recreation Area, CA

CAMERON + COMPANY PETALUMA CA 94952 WWW.CAMERONBOOKS.COM

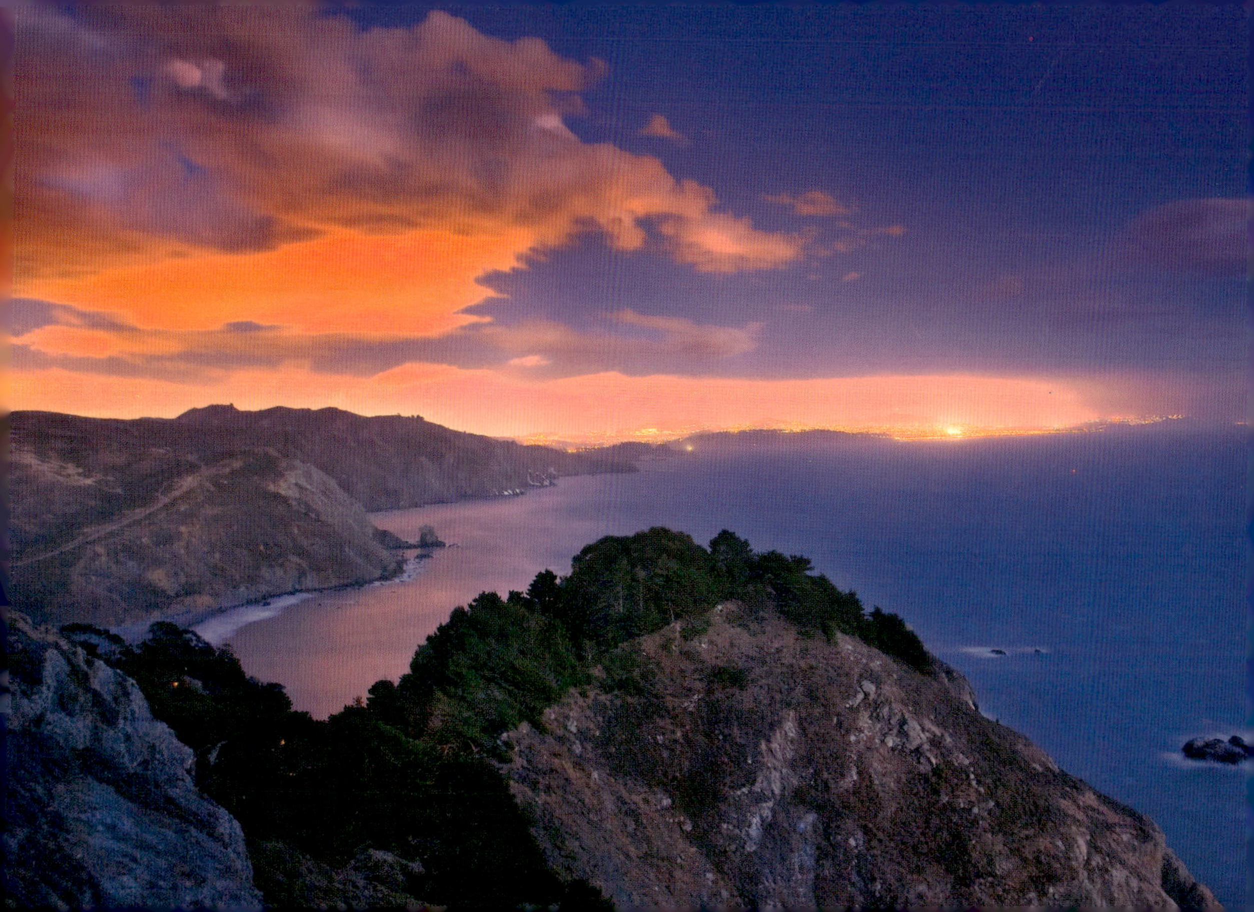

Point Reyes and the Marin Headlands

San Francisco and the Marin Headlands from Muir Beach Overlook, Golden Gate National Recreation Area, CA

CAMERON + COMPANY PETALUMA CA 94952 WWW.CAMERONBOOKS.COM

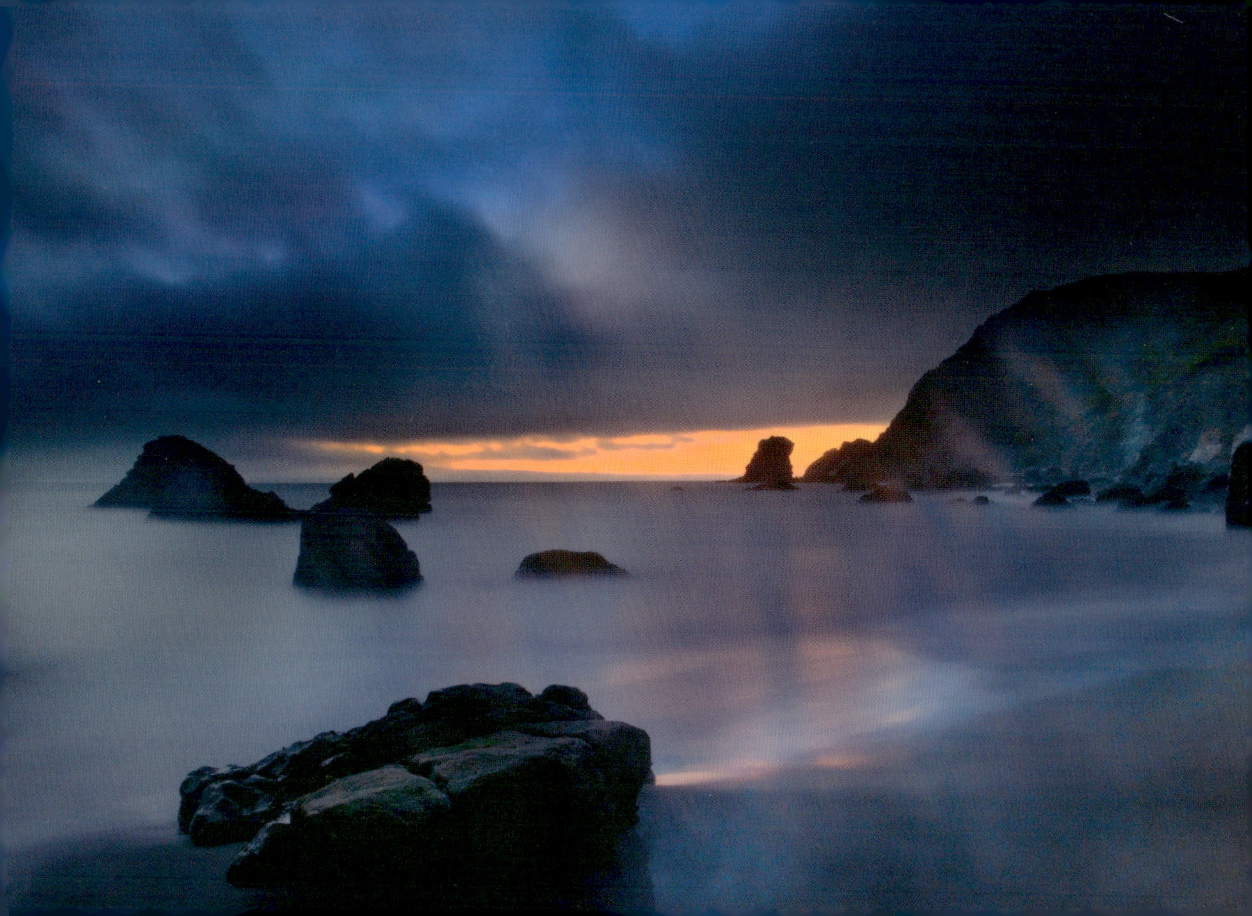

Point Reyes and the Marin Headlands

Dusk at Pirate's Cove, Golden Gate National Recreation Area, CA

CAMERON + COMPANY PETALUMA CA 94952 WWW.CAMERONBOOKS.COM

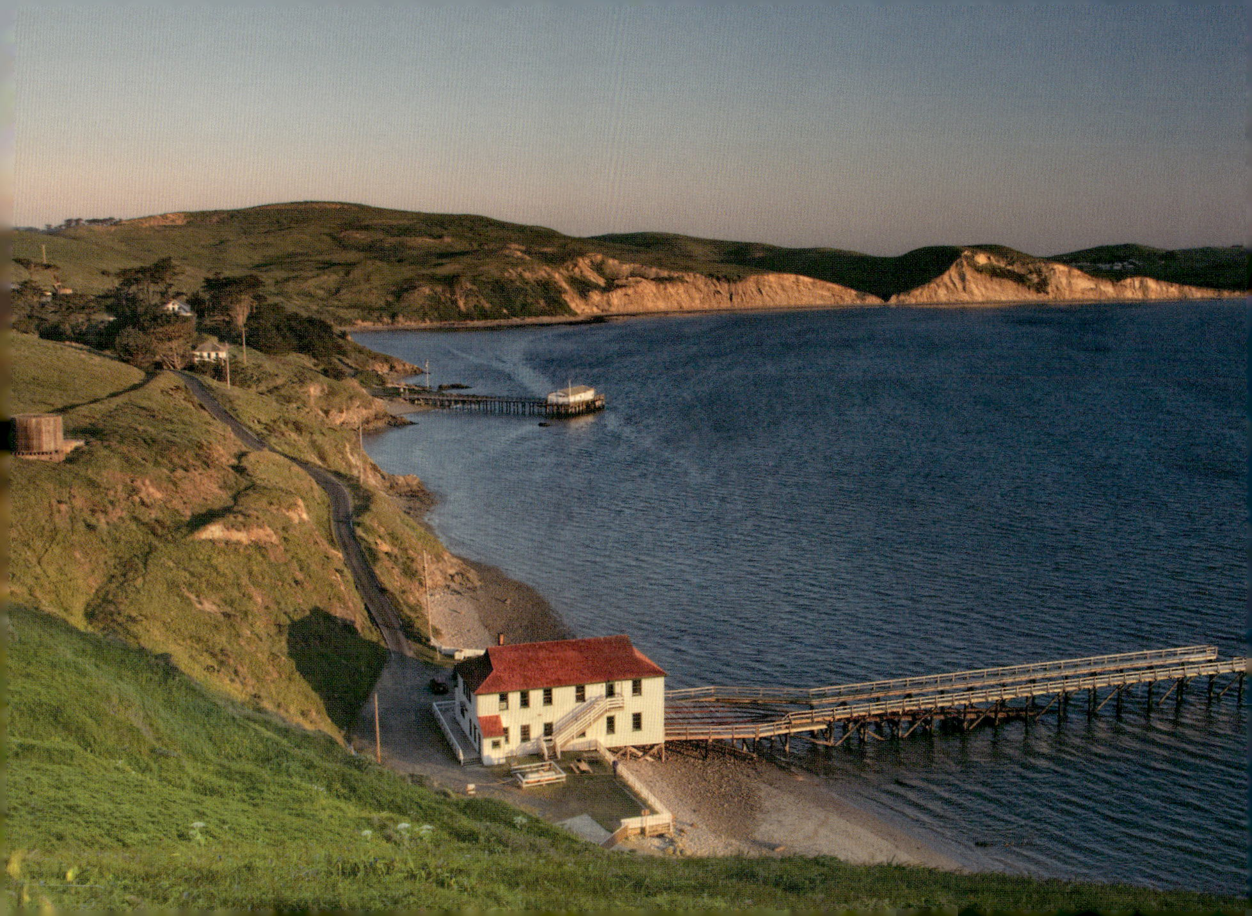

Point Reyes and the Marin Headlands

Point Reyes Morning—Drakes Bay and the historic Coastguard Boathouse, Point Reyes National Seashore, CA

CAMERON + COMPANY PETALUMA CA 94952 WWW.CAMERONBOOKS.COM

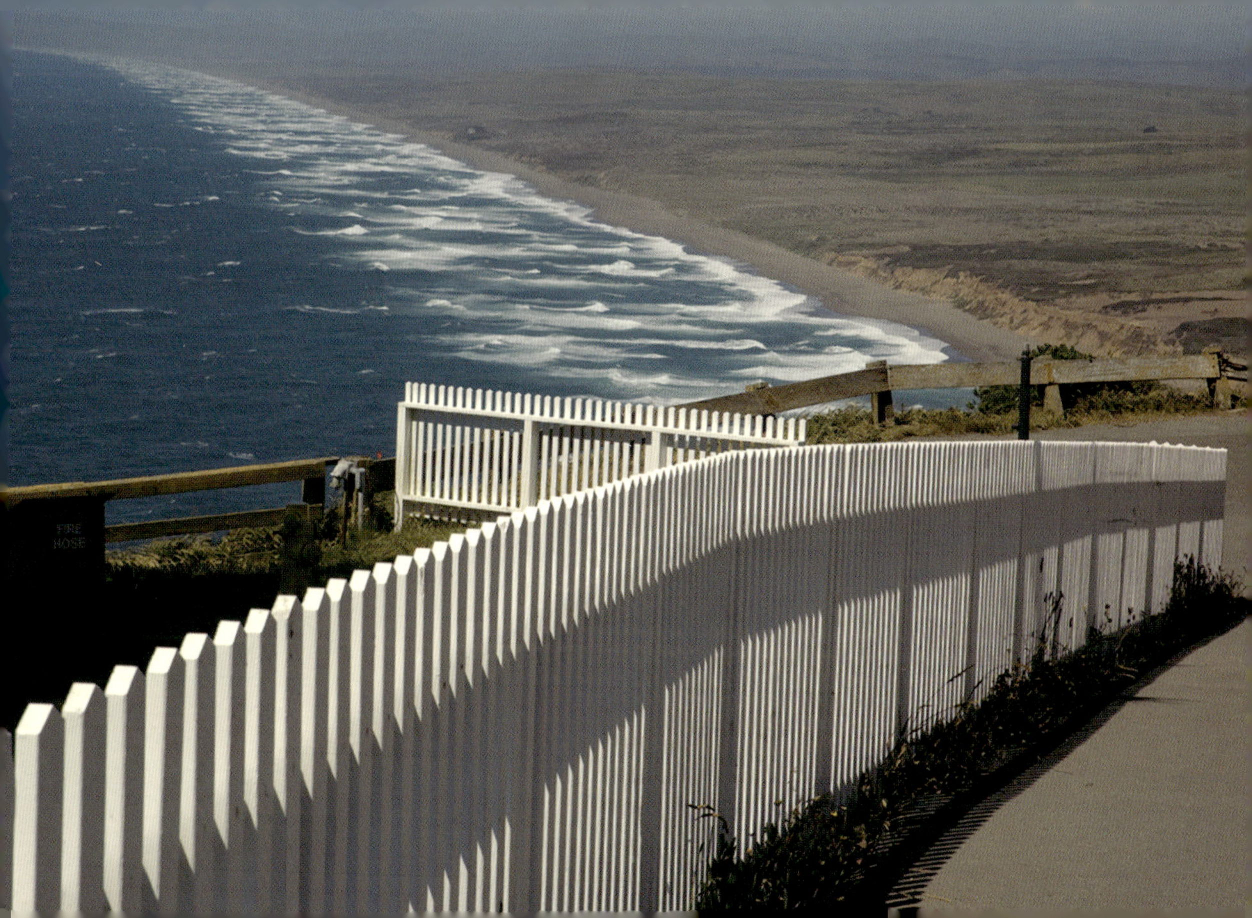

Point Reyes and the Marin Headlands

White Fence—with the Great Beach behind,
Point Reyes National Seashore, CA

CAMERON + COMPANY PETALUMA CA 94952 WWW.CAMERONBOOKS.COM

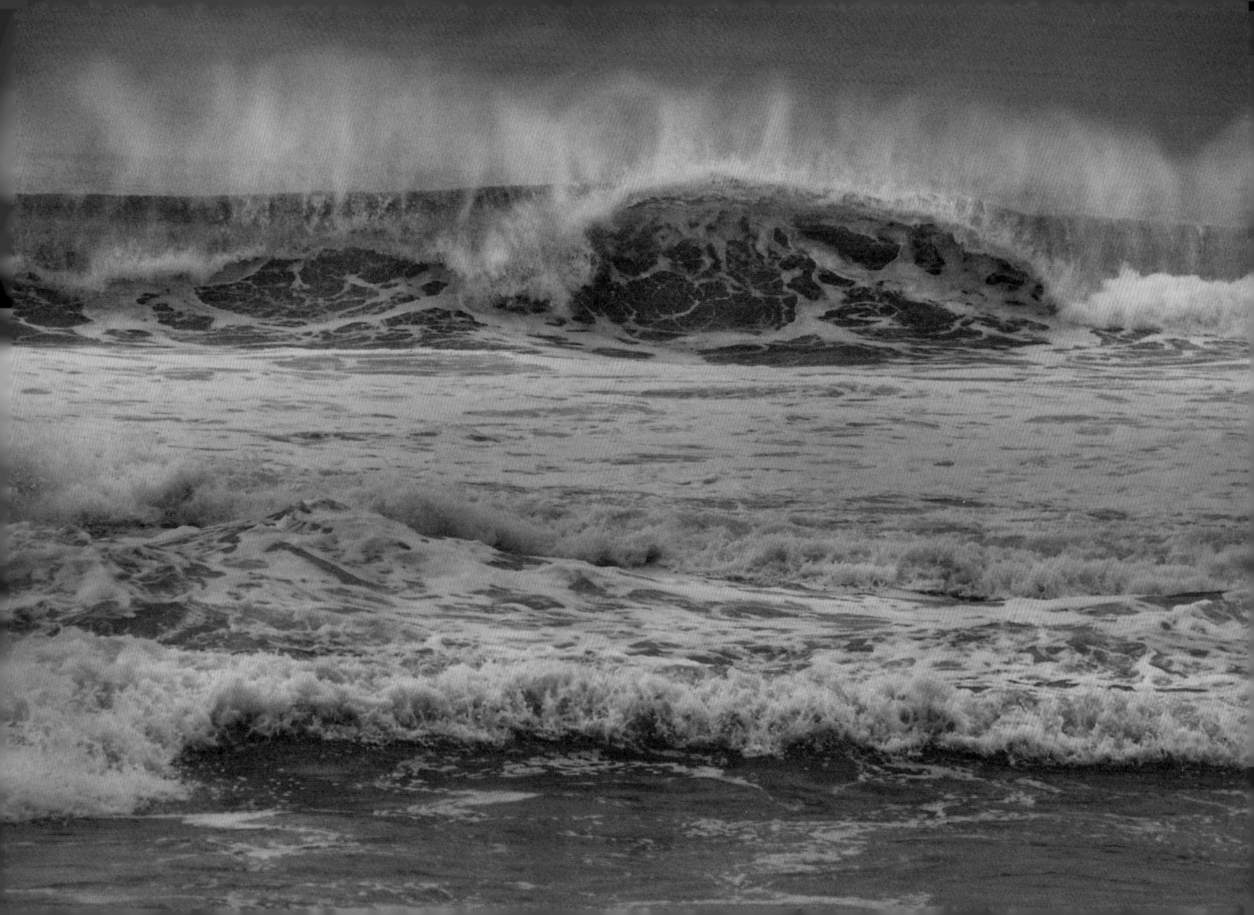

Point Reyes and the Marin Headlands

Waves—Winter Surf on South Beach,
Point Reyes National Seashore, CA

CAMERON + COMPANY PETALUMA CA 94952 WWW.CAMERONBOOKS.COM

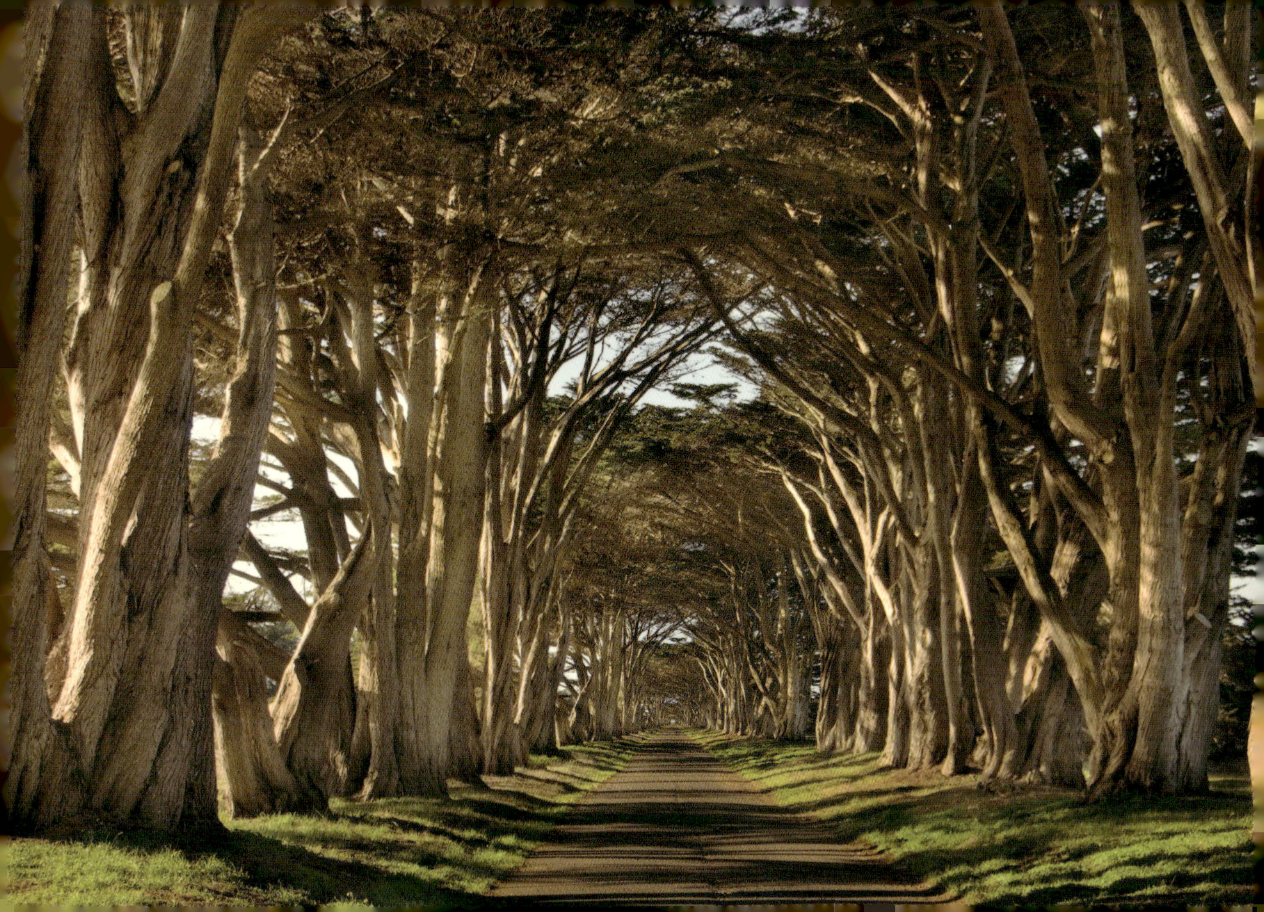

Point Reyes and the Marin Headlands

Monterey Pines—leading to the historic Marconi Broadcast Station, Point Reyes National Seashore, CA

CAMERON + COMPANY PETALUMA CA 94952 WWW.CAMERONBOOKS.COM

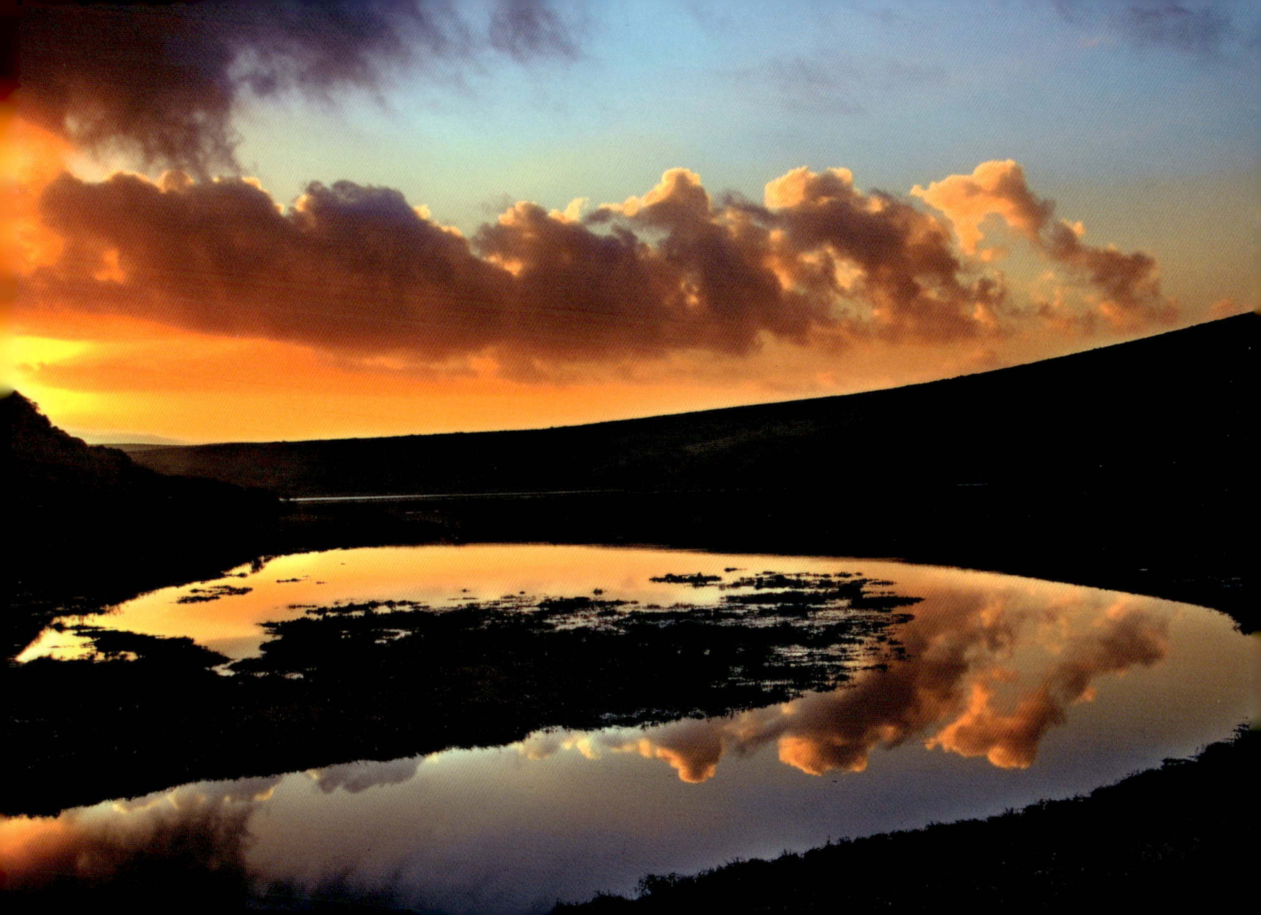

Point Reyes and the Marin Headlands

Drakes Estero, Point Reyes National Seashore, CA

CAMERON + COMPANY PETALUMA CA 94952 WWW.CAMERONBOOKS.COM

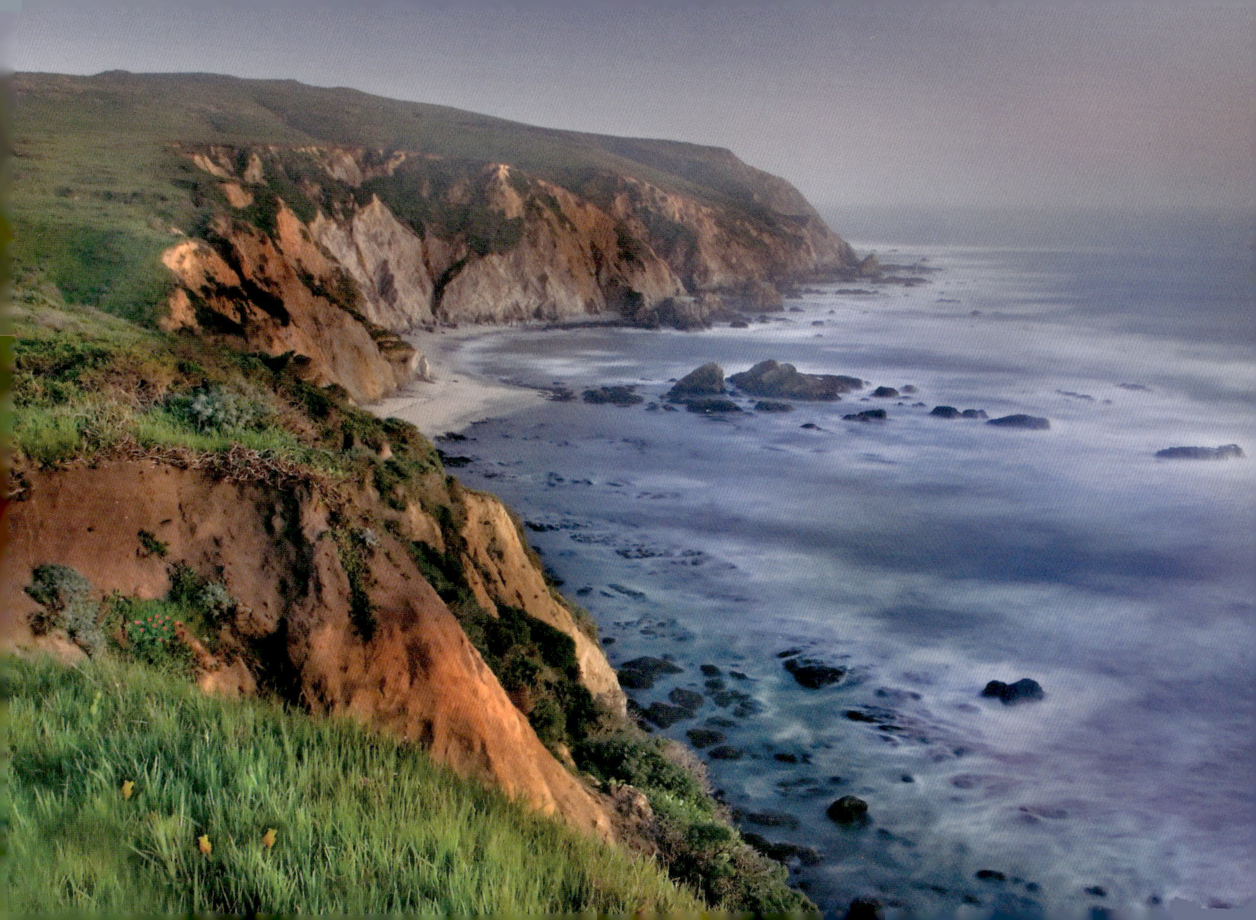

Point Reyes and the Marin Headlands

Tomales Point, Point Reyes National Seashore, CA

CAMERON + COMPANY PETALUMA CA 94952 WWW.CAMERONBOOKS.COM

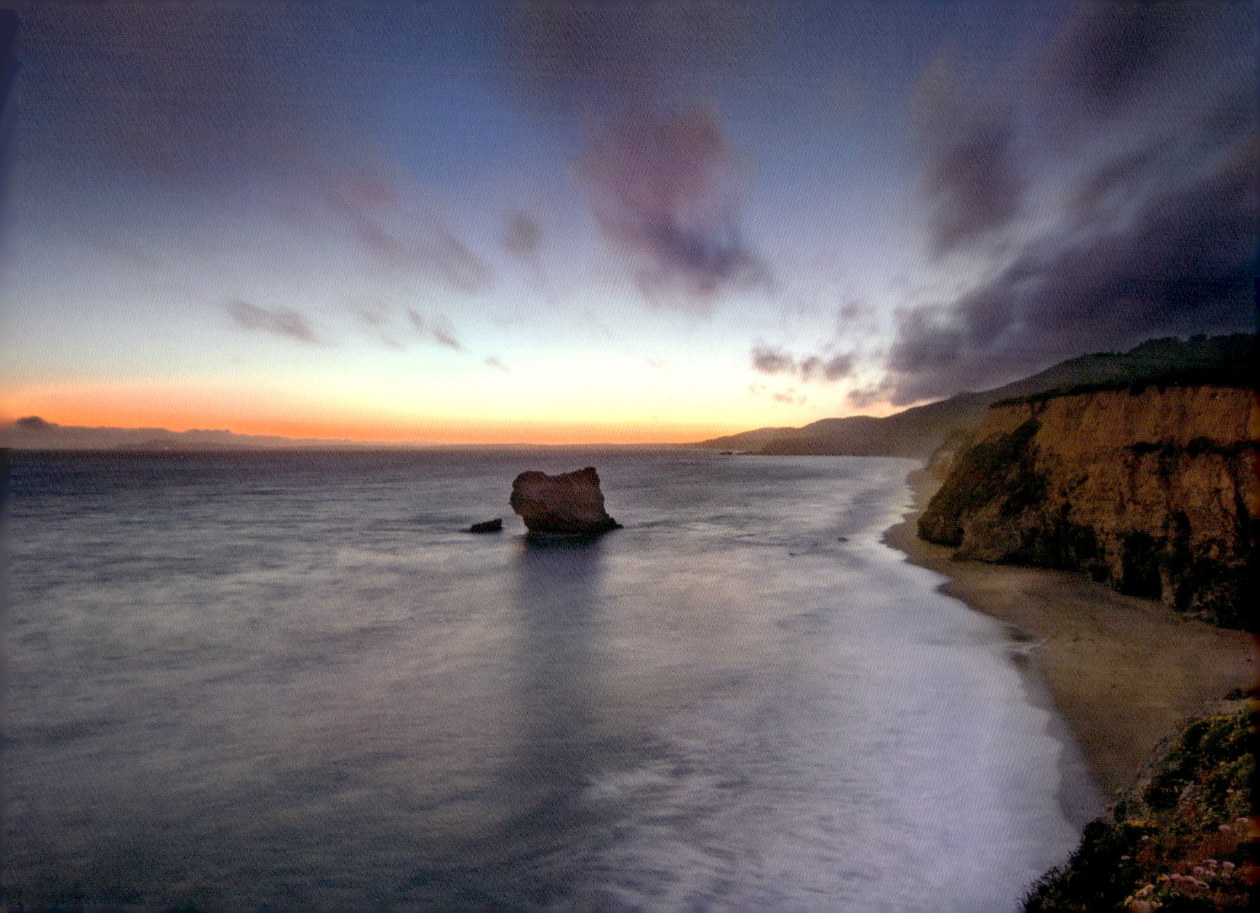

Point Reyes and the Marin Headlands

Point Reyes from Arch Rock, Point Reyes National Seashore, CA

CAMERON + COMPANY PETALUMA CA 94952 WWW.CAMERONBOOKS.COM

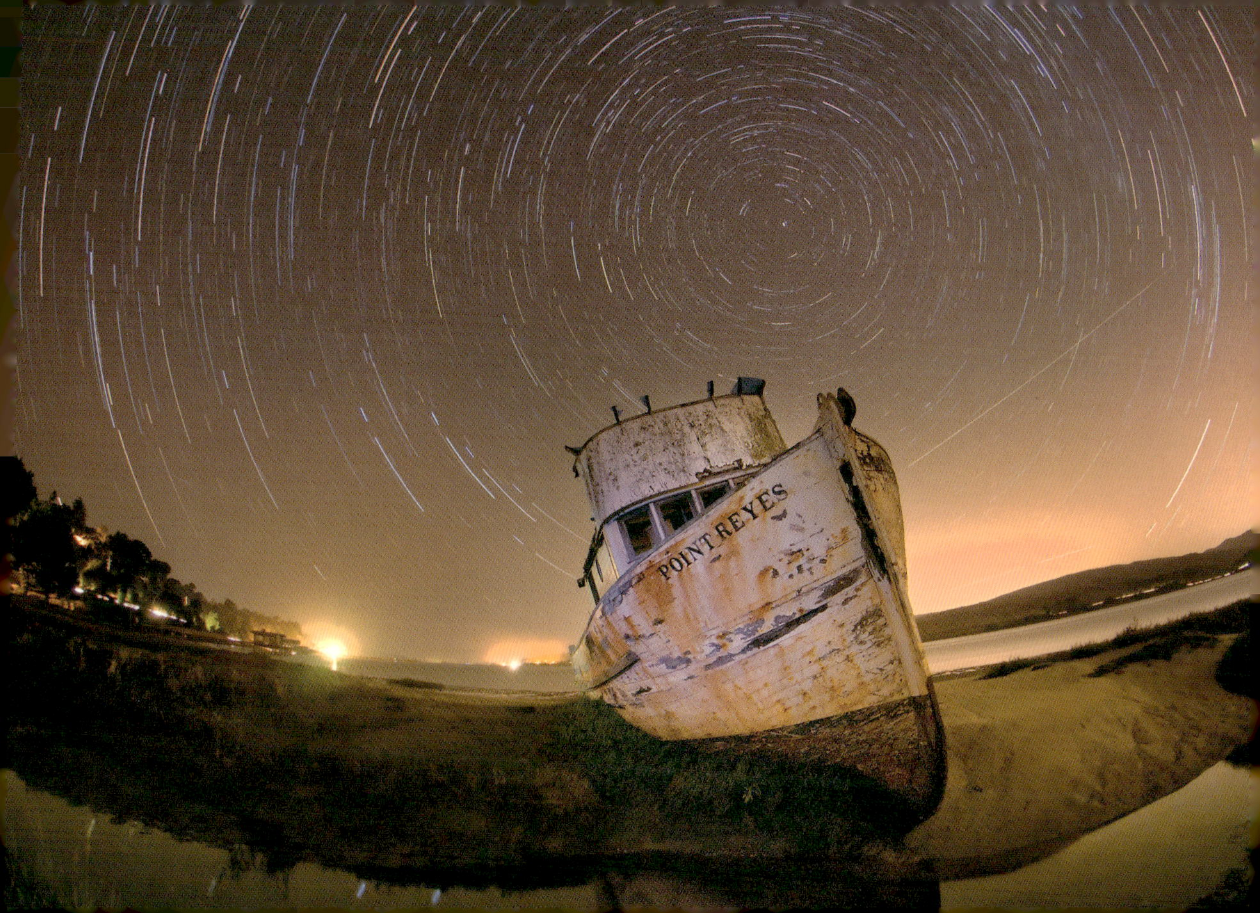
POINT REYES

Point Reyes and the Marin Headlands

Between Earth and Sky—Point Reyes trawler, Inverness, CA

CAMERON + COMPANY PETALUMA CA 94952 WWW.CAMERONBOOKS.COM

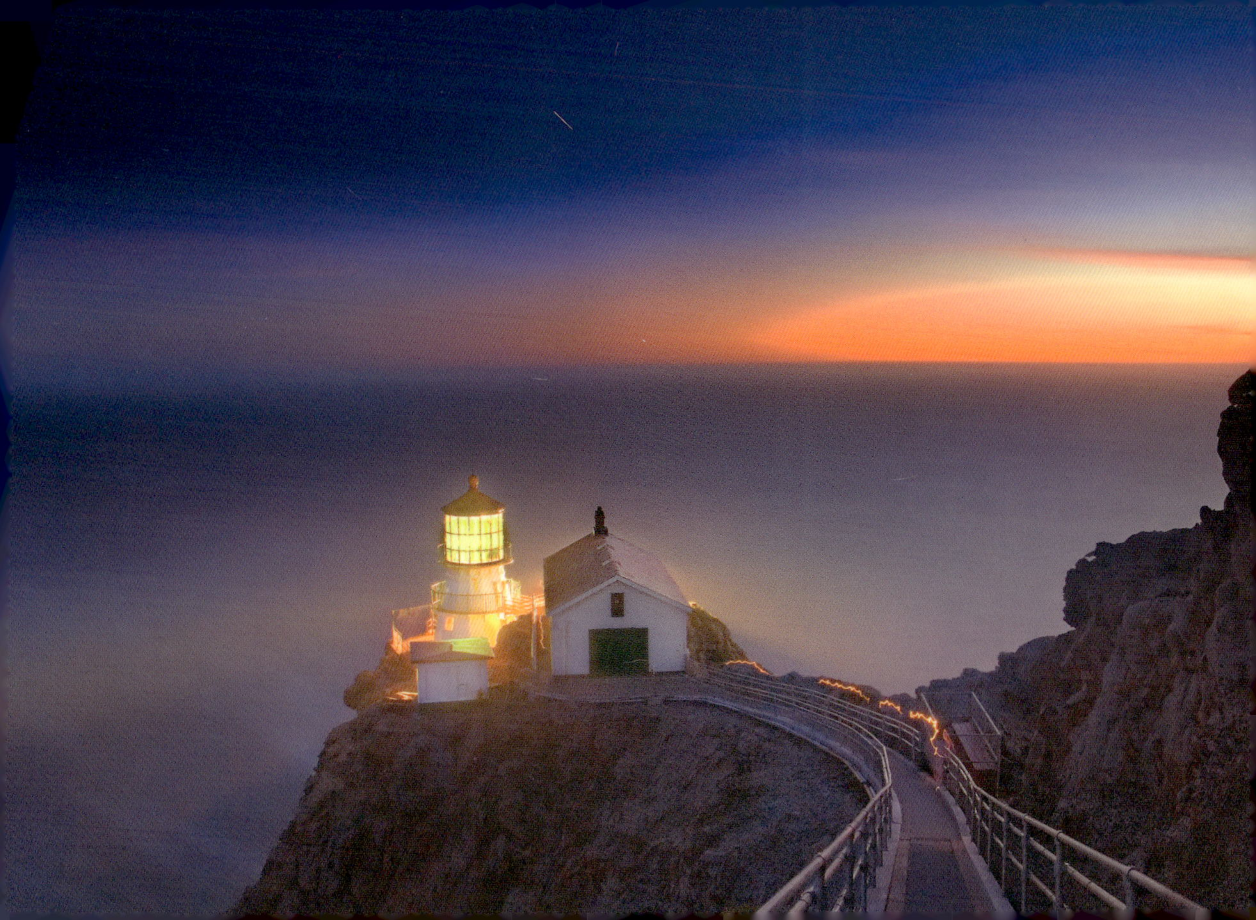

Point Reyes and the Marin Headlands

Night at Point Reyes Lighthouse, Point Reyes National Seashore, CA

CAMERON + COMPANY PETALUMA CA 94952 WWW.CAMERONBOOKS.COM